Through Creative Eyes

Amy Cook

BookLeaf
Publishing

India | USA | UK

Presentation by *BookLeaf Publishing*

Web: www.bookleafpub.com

E-mail: info@bookleafpub.com

ISBN:9789358315332

First edition 2024

DEDICATION

To John Cook, my Grandad, whilst you may be gone, your creativity lives in me. No matter how much time has passed, I can still hear you telling me to always think outside the box. I may not have understood then, but all your tidbits of advice finally make sense. I love you, and yes, 'Tempus Fugit'. Time Flies, even when we aren't having fun.

ACKNOWLEDGEMENT

I want to first thank my family for never giving up on my dreams and always finding ways to encourage my creativity. I want to thank BookLeaf Publishing for giving me the opportunity to share my work with anyone who wishes to read it and for giving me the motivation I needed to keep on writing. I would also like to thank anyone who decides to give my poems a chance, as without the readers of the world, I would not have an audience to express my creativity to begin with.

PREFACE

As an author, I intend to bring joy and a new perspective to various topics; while I may describe what I see, think, and feel within my poems, this does not mean everyone will see what I have tried to paint a picture of. The point of these poems is, in fact, to prove that not everyone has the same perspective and that thinking outside of the box can often be fun and even helpful within the right circumstances.

The Midnight Prowler

Stalking through the field at night,
Predatory gaze to cause a fright,
Claws raked soil and shredded grass,
Paws are sturdy; made to last.

Muscles rippled as it prowled,
It's prey scattered as it growled,
Not the animal you'd expect,
But a tabby…. a household pet.

Trevor The Temporary Traffic Light

Trevor the temporary traffic light here,
How do you do?
I know you can see me,
I can see you too.
You're at the front of the queue again,
I caught you yesterday,
If I had my own way,
I'd let you on your way.
See the men behind me?
Between me and you,
I don't think they have anything better to do.
Anyway, let's get back to me and you.
You called me a very rude name when you
missed the last bright green,
I think you are quite horrid and the slightest
mean
But cause I'm nice and happy,
I'll let you off Scott clean!
So, we've got a few things straight now.
And it's not going to happen again!
If I see you yet again,
In front of the colour red,
I'll remember to put happy thoughts,
Right inside your head.

So remember, dear kind driver,
You can see me,
I can see you,
And one little thing,
Patience is a virtue.

Where I'd Rather Be

Where I'd rather be,
It's a choice that's so easy!

Up a mountain
In a fountain,
On a plane
France or Spain
That's where I'd rather be!

Where I'd rather be than here,
Is all quite easy, crystal clear!

In a volcano
The wild with a rhino,
In a pool
But not in a school!
That's where I'd rather be!

Where I'd rather be,
All the above is a fantasy!

Where I'd really like to go,
Is to my warm and friendly,
Very own home!

Spring

Snow is melting off the mountains,
Precious flowers start their sprouting,
Radiant green leaves on the trees,
Intelligent birds migrating, you will see,
New life flourishing, spreading cheer,
Gone is Winter... Spring is here!

Summer

Sweltering heat,
Sandy Feet,
Melting Ice-Cream
Children beam,
Swimming pools,
Days off school,
Having Fun,
In the sun,
Suntan Lines,
Parking Fines,

All through Summer,
There's nothing funner.

Autumn

Days are slowly getting shorter,
Pumpkin Spice's biggest supporter,
Cosy days curled by the fire,
Long, warm coats are the best attire.

Orange and red are the constant hues,
The perfect excuse to buy new boots,
Leaves are falling all around us,
Squirrels rush to forage nuts.

An introvert's favourite time of year,
Autumn is upon us; inside, we disappear.

Winter

Condensation made from your breath,
Icy roads make you fear death,
Darkest days of all the year,
Spending time with those most dear.

Everyone is filled with holiday spirit,
Hot drinks are made for those who visit,
Heating on, windows are closed,
Look outside! It's clearly snowed!

Love Is Not A Strong Enough Word

Lost without you, I would be,
I care for you like you're family,
Consuming me from head to toe,
How I lived before you, I will never know.

I feel it all inside my chest
Something I cannot express,
Words could never show how much,
I think I'd starve without your touch,

The need to tell you always burns,
But at the end of the day,
Actions speak louder than words.

You Can Take Comfort In Me

A friend for life is what this is,
A comfort item that lasts for years,
Soft and gentle, in many shapes,
It makes you feel better after any scrapes.

A gentle face and rounded ears,
One quick hold melts all your fears,
It's stuffed and squishy and great for hugs,
Something that won't deny you belly rubs.

It helps anyone who touches it fall asleep,
Something to clutch when you have to weep,
No matter your age, your race, your gender,
A teddy bear is a comfort that lasts forever.

A Night Of Colourful Noise

BOOM! Woosh, Fizz,
It's always the way it is.

CRASH! Crackle, Sparkle,
The noise will make you startle.

BANG! Swoop, Ting,
Joy is what they bring.

CLANG! Swirl, Flash,
A few seconds is all it lasts

ZOOM! Shoot, Soar,
With fireworks, we always want more.

Christmas

Snowmen, sledging, socks and sweaters,
Christmas trees and Santa letters,
Hot chocolate, marshmallows, gingerbread
houses,
Spending time with family and spouses,
Christmas movies and wrapping gifts,
Yes, my child Santa exists,
Cosy fires and huge blankets,
Last-minute sorting of gift baskets,

Winter may be dark and cold,
But the magic of Christmas does not get old.

The Two Budgies

Eric and Russel, two budgies in a cage,
Eric's very happy, but Russel's in a rage,
They've been stuck in a cage all day,
With nothing to do and nothing to play.

Did I tell you an amazing fact?
Eric weighs ten tonnes and is very fat.
So fancy that,
A ten-tonne budgie!
It's no wonder Russel's grumpy.

When It Rains

I always want to run outside,
Find a place on the ground and lie,
Feel it patter on my skin,
Laugh at the joy I feel within,
Let the water wash away,
The negatives, until I feel okay,
Let the rain cleanse my soul,
Until I feel I have control.

Even the sky needs release,
To let the pressure merely cease,
To let the rain wash away,
Everything I feel today.

The Guilt Of Relief

When you lose someone you care about,
You feel lost and sad, I have no doubt,
But something else you may feel,
Is guilty of the relief that's revealed.

Not relief for the death or loss of love,
But for the relief you have just because,
They may be gone, but not forgotten,
But relief for the fact they don't feel rotten,
The pain they felt has gone away,
They will not suffer for one more day.

Your loss will stay with you forever,
You may feel pain for them, however,
They are at peace now, that's for sure,
They are not in pain anymore.

Dont be guilty over feeling relief,
Because even though they are gone, they are at
peace,
You would not wish them any pain,
Even if it meant never seeing them again.

Readers Can Be Anything

You read a book to get away,
From the real world if just for one day.

You can fight a dragon and fall in love,
Have wings of gold and fly above,
Have magic powers and wield a sword,
Buy a fancy car you can't afford.

All by reading a few words,
A couple of adjectives maybe some verbs,
The words are put on simple paper,
But a reader's mind makes it something greater,
With a book and the imagination of someone,
They can turn themselves into anyone.

Sleeping

Some people dream when they fall asleep,
Others cannot make themselves relax so deep.
Dreams for some are extremely vivid,
Whereas others sleep like they aren't living.

Rarer still are insomniacs,
Who cannot sleep and cannot nap,
They struggle through daily tasks,
And stay awake until they collapse.

Not one person sleeps the same,
Even if 8 hours is the aim,
Some people toss and turn all night,
While others would sleep through their house
alight.

Sleep is needed by every person,
That is a fact, I am certain,
So try and sleep whichever way,
That helps you start another day.

Depression Is Not Just Being Sad

It is not always crying yourself to sleep,
Sometimes, you can't bring yourself to eat,
You feel drained and always tired,
But at the same time, you feel wired.

Depression isn't just feeling sad,
You feel crazy, raging mad,
Angry at the slightest thing,
Snap so easily like a string.

Overwhelmed and feeling down,
Normal tasks make you feel drowned,
Having a shower is too much,
Wanting love but hating touch.

Depression isn't just being sad,
You feel crazy, you're going mad,
Yes, you cry and hide in bed,
But you're mostly trapped right in your head.

Duckie The Duck

There once was a duck called Duckie,
He thought himself very lucky!

That was until,
The restaurant on the hill,
Turned him into Kentucky!

I'm A Giraffe

I'm a Giraffe,
My neck is so long,
If I stretched it all out,
It would reach to Hong Kong!

Trevor The Temporary Traffic Light: The Good And The Bad

Trevor the temporary traffic light,
Is not very bright,
He makes the traffic wait a lot
That's his bad side.

When he's green, everybody is happy,
When he's red, they're all annoyed,
He keeps everybody waiting,
Which causes lots of noise.

This poem is short for a reason,
To get a point across.

The only good thing about Trevor,
Is if he's broken or he's off.

The Skateboarding Duck

I know you've all heard about the skateboarding
duck,
But I've just been told he ran out of luck!
It happened on Wednesday,
The week before last.
He was going down a hill far too fast!
When he hit a bump,
And came down with a crash.

Now he's being served,
With dumplings and mash!